breaking
FREE FROM
busyness

ALEXA HESS

Busyness often reveals how we are slaves to our schedules instead of servants of our Savior.

Part One: The Problem

Day 1 Addressing Chronic Busyness 8

Day 2 Busyness & Our Walk with God 12

Day 3 Busyness & Our Relationships With Others 16

Day 4 Busyness & Our Health 20

Day 5 Using Our Time for God's Glory 24

Part Two: Priorities

Day 6 Why the Right Priorities Matter 30

Day 7 God 34

Day 8 Family 38

Day 9 Church & Christian Fellowship 42

Day 10 Work 46

Day 11 Service 50

Day 12 Stewardship 54

Day 13 Self-Care 58

Part Three: Making a Plan

Day 14 Evaluating Our Time 64

Day 15 Setting Goals 70

Day 16 Establishing Boundaries 74

Day 17 Pursuing Accountability 78

Day 18 Putting It All Together 82

Part Four: Truth to Remember

Day 19 You Are Not Limitless   92

Day 20 You Are Not in Control   96

Day 21 You Are Not Omnipresent   100

Day 22 The Importance of Rest   104

Day 23 The Importance of Stillness   108

Day 24 The Importance of Prayer   112

Day 25 The Importance of Bible Study   116

Day 26 It's Okay to Say "No"   120

Day 27 It's Okay to Slow Down   124

Day 28 It's Okay to Ask for Help   128

Part Five: Wrapping Up

Day 29 Our Time in Light of Eternity   134

Day 30 Reflection   138

PART ONE

The Problem

Day 1   Addressing Chronic Busyness

Day 2   Busyness & Our Walk with God

Day 3   Busyness & Our Relationship with Others

Day 4   Busyness & Our Health

Day 5   Using Our Time for God's Glory

Addressing Chronic Busyness

How do you respond when people ask how you are? For many of us, "busy" is the word that first slips out. Our fast-paced culture influences us to move from one thing to the next so often that it can feel as if we live in perpetual motion. But with busyness often being perceived as a mark of success, we might not think it is bad to live this way. However, there are negative aspects to busyness. A jam-packed schedule can cause us to neglect our families and friends, keep us from prioritizing our spiritual growth, and lead to stress and burnout.

Yet we often push down this reality because we feel like busyness is part of life. With work, appointments, events, and necessary daily tasks, it seems as if always doing and never resting is normal. While busyness is natural for certain days or specific seasons, chronic busyness is dangerous. When we allow ourselves to be too busy at the expense of our relationships and spiritual and mental health, busyness becomes a problem, perhaps even an idol. If we do not consider how we are using our time, we may be going and going but never truly living.

As followers of Christ, we are to live our lives for the Lord. Yet busyness often reveals how we are slaves to our schedules instead of servants of our Savior. As believers, it is not about having a busy life but a fruitful life. The difference lies in what we allow to motivate our actions. If we live for ourselves or for the world, we will approach our time with a desire for success, security, and satisfaction. But if we live for Christ, we will approach our time with a desire for faithfulness.

This thirty-day challenge allows you to evaluate if and how busyness has become a problem in your life. It will enable you to change your habits and priorities to help you move from chronic busyness to a fruitful and gospel-centered life. We will achieve this goal in five parts. Part one, covered over the next four days, will focus on the importance of living for God's glory and how chronic busyness can distract us from living for God's glory. Part two will speak to the priorities we should have as followers of Christ, and part three will help you make a plan to use your time well. Lastly, part four will provide truths and encouragement as you put your plan into action, and part five will allow you to reflect on your executed plan.

As you go through this challenge, remember that each one of us fails to use our time well in one way or another. If you are in Christ, Christ's grace covers these mistakes and failures. So rest in Christ's grace as you evaluate your life, make a plan, and rely on His strength within you that empowers you to live for Him. Most of all, remember that it is not a perfect schedule that secures your favor with God but the perfect grace of Christ.

It is not a perfect schedule that secures your favor with God but the perfect grace of Christ.

Write out a prayer below, asking for God's help as you partake in this challenge. Ask Him to open your eyes to the changes you need to make in your life and give you the strength to make those changes. Ask Him to help you rest in His grace as you go through this challenge.

Busyness & Our Walk with God

Your alarm goes off, and your day begins. You prepare your kids' lunches for school, make sure your children are dressed, and cook a quick breakfast. You notice your Bible on the shelf and think, *I'll read it when I get home*. After dropping your kids off at school, you come home and notice the mess your kids left behind from breakfast. Once you clean up that mess, you remember the massive pile of laundry you need to wash. *I'll read my Bible once the laundry is in the wash*, you think. But as soon as the washing machine starts running, your phone rings, and your daughter says she left her homework at home. You drive back to the school, drop off the homework, and run into a mom who asks if you can volunteer at a bake sale tomorrow. You say yes, and now you have signed yourself up to bake forty cupcakes. When the day is done and you are cleaning up from dinner and your cupcakes are baking, it hits you that you did not read your Bible. *I'll do it tomorrow*, you commit to yourself.

Does this situation sound familiar? Even if the events in this situation do not connect exactly with your life, it is likely that you have had moments when you pushed off Bible reading because of your schedule. It is easy for us to believe that we do not have time to read, pray, or prioritize other spiritual disciplines in our lives. We joke that there are "not enough hours in the day" and think that if only we had more time, then we would be able to fit in prayer or Bible reading. But the more our Bibles collect dust on the shelf, the more our hearts grow callous to God and His Word.

We might not think this is true because the symptoms of this reality can be subtle. We lash out at our family or friends, go to bed overwhelmed, and find ourselves easily distraught from even the smallest setback. These feelings and actions might reveal that we have not soaked up time in God's presence. While our world motivates us to fill our schedules, God's Word calls us to fill our hearts. When we focus on fitting as much as we can into our days over caring for the spiritual condition of our hearts, we keep ourselves from growing in godliness.

As followers of Christ, we cannot live without time spent with God and His Word. Without God, we can do nothing. Even if we feel like we are accomplishing much in our day-to-day lives, all we accomplish is due to God and His grace. So let us recognize our need for the Lord and our utter dependence on Him. May we choose to prioritize walking with God over our to-do lists. The spiritual condition of our hearts matters, and when we make the time to fill our hearts, we will live faithful rather than frazzled lives.

" WHILE OUR WORLD MOTIVATES US TO FILL OUR SCHEDULES, GOD'S WORD CALLS US TO FILL OUR HEARTS.

May we choose to prioritize walking with God over our to-do lists.

---

1. *Why is your spiritual health important?*

....

....

....

....

....

....

2. *How is your spiritual health being impacted by busyness?*

....

....

....

....

....

....

3. *How does busyness take away from your relationship with God?*

....

....

....

....

....

....

Busyness & Our Relationships with Others

A little boy approaches his dad with a baseball glove and asks if he can play catch with him. "Not now," the dad says to the boy, "I have to mow the lawn." A text message flashes across a woman's phone, saying, "Hey! I haven't heard from you in a while; how are you?" The woman glances at the message and turns her phone over, resolving to respond when she has a free moment. A husband sits at a restaurant and checks his watch. His wife is thirty minutes late to their scheduled dinner date because she stayed late at work.

Our busyness does not only affect our relationship with God but also our relationships with others. We might not believe this to be true, but if we took a step back to examine our lives, we would likely see areas where busyness has impacted our friends and families. We miss out on our kids' recitals or sports games because of tasks we have added to our schedules. We allow the days to pass without making any effort to connect with a family member or friend. Our full schedules cause us to lose our sense of connection with our spouses.

While there are seasons of life when our schedules are naturally more full than others, and there are obligations we must commit to, we can add things to our days without considering how they affect our relationships with others. If we do not take the time to consider how our busyness affects others, we can create distance between our friends and us, bring tension into our marriages, and neglect our little ones.

God built us to be relational. In His intentional design that reflects the beauty of the Trinity, God made us to be communal people who need each other. He gifted us with friends, marriages, and family so that we could do life together. When we focus more on our schedules than our relationships, we neglect God's gift of community. Busyness often prevents us from pouring out our love, care, and support to others and receiving love, care, and support in return. Busyness can also fuel the sin of pride, convincing us that we can be self-reliant and self-sufficient people.

Today's reading may already be exposing areas of your life where your busyness has negatively impacted others. While it may be painful to have these areas exposed, it is good to be aware of them. It is far better to bring these issues to light rather than remain blind to the damage our busyness may be creating. Naturally, having your sins and failures exposed might make you feel ashamed. But instead of crumbling in shame over the ways you may have neglected your relationships, rest in Christ's grace and allow His grace to motivate change. You need others as others need you, and with the help of the Spirit, you can prioritize your friends and family and prevent busyness from hurting the relationships God has gifted you.

When we focus more on our schedules than our relationships, we neglect God's gift of community.

1. *Why are your relationships with others important?*

....

....

....

....

....

2. *Who are the main relationships in your life?*

....

....

....

....

....

3. *How have you seen busyness affect your relationships with these people?*

....

....

....

....

....

Busyness &
Our Health

A recent study found that sixty-four percent of Americans say they do not have time to take care of themselves. Would you say that this is true for yourself? We might know that our health is important but feel as if our schedules do not allow us the time we need to prioritize exercise, healthy eating, and sleep. It is easy to make excuses for our health because of a supposed lack of time. Yet we might tell ourselves we will exercise when we get off work—only to come home and spend the evening sitting on the couch and watching our favorite show. Or we might wake up thinking that today is the day we are going to eat clean, only to run through the drive-thru on our way to work. Just as it is for our relationship with God and others, busyness negatively affects our health in subtle ways.

We can lay awake at night, consumed with tomorrow's to-do list. We can chug cup after cup of coffee to receive enough energy to get through the day. Even when we have a day off, we might feel stressed and unable to relax, thinking about what we should be doing with our time until we return to work. Neglecting the health of our bodies due to busyness is dangerous. If we are not careful, the stress that often accompanies busyness can lead to anxiety, high blood pressure, and possibly even heart problems.

God gifted us with our bodies, and we are to steward the bodies He has given us well. First Corinthians 6:19–20 tells us, "Don't you know that your body is a temple of the Holy Spirit who is in you, whom you have from God? You are not your own, for you were bought at a price. So glorify God with your body." Even though these verses are about sexual immorality, they remind us that our bodies are vessels of worship. If we are in Christ, the Holy Spirit indwells us, which makes our bodies living temples. We glorify God by caring for the bodies He has entrusted to us. While there will certainly be days and seasons in which we cannot prioritize our health as we so desire, we can still aim to glorify God by caring for ourselves, even in the smallest ways.

Though we might not think we have enough time to care for our health, we do. We should not wait until we burn out or receive a medical diagnosis to start taking care of ourselves. Prioritizing our health will require intentionality and discipline, but we can create opportunities within our schedules for regular exercise, healthy eating, and rest. And with the help of the Holy Spirit, we receive the strength we need to change unhealthy habits and remain disciplined in our health. As we aim to glorify God and rely on the power of the Spirit, we will steward the bodies God has given us.

> JUST AS IT IS FOR OUR RELATIONSHIP WITH GOD AND OTHERS, BUSYNESS NEGATIVELY AFFECTS OUR HEALTH IN SUBTLE WAYS.

We glorify God by caring for the bodies He has entrusted to us.

1. *What are some unhealthy habits you have developed due to busyness?*

....

....

....

....

....

2. *How have you seen busyness negatively impact your health?*

....

....

....

....

....

3. *How does the truth that your body is for God's glory encourage you to prioritize your health?*

....

....

....

....

....

Using Our Time for God's Glory

Over the past several days, we have looked at how busyness can affect our walk with God, our relationships with others, and our health. If we find that our schedules are keeping us from prioritizing our relationship with the Lord, investing in our friends and families, and taking care of our health, it is possible that our schedules have been centered around us rather than the Lord. Taking our focus away from God and placing it on ourselves or other things apart from Him keeps us from living obediently to the Lord. When we fill our schedules with things, even good things, but are not living out what God's Word commands and teaches, we are not glorifying the Lord as we should.

Paul explains how we should do everything for God's glory when he writes, "So, whether you eat or drink, or whatever you do, do everything for the glory of God" (1 Corinthians 10:31). We are to give God glory through everything we do, and this includes how we use our time. However, it is possible to fill our time with things that we believe will give God glory only to end up perpetuating busyness in our lives. We might even make excuses for our busyness because we are filling our schedules with activities and commitments that seem like they are worshipful to the Lord. The issue here is that we can allow our motivation to accomplish God-glorifying things to keep us from being obedient to God's other commands (Matthew 5–7, 22:37–39). Our overloaded schedules may be filled with things we hope will give God glory, but those things can take us away from rest, family, and spiritual disciplines.

A packed schedule can also reveal a prideful heart. Even the tasks and roles that bring God glory can be executed with a self-centered attitude. We can end up saying yes to things in order to feel needed by others. We can believe that we are capable of taking on multiple tasks at once to prove we can handle them on our own. Because of this, a schedule full of good things can end up being more about ourselves than the Lord. But when we give God the glory He deserves, our schedules will reflect our worship. Our devotion to Him and our focus on Him will be evident in the way we use our time to serve God.

In the next section, we will continue to do some heart work by evaluating our priorities. But for now, stop and consider whether you are currently using your time for God's glory above all else. Think through the motivation for your work, tasks, and roles. Consider whether you are doing too much, and examine your true motives. God is worthy of our worship, and we live with intentionality when we focus on glorifying Him. It is when God sits on the throne of our hearts that our time will be fruitful and reflective of the God we serve.

> **WE ARE TO GIVE GOD GLORY THROUGH EVERYTHING WE DO, AND THIS INCLUDES HOW WE USE OUR TIME.**

When we give
God the glory
He deserves,
our schedules
will reflect
our worship.

1. *Why are we supposed to give God glory?*

....

....

....

....

2. *Why is it easy to think we are glorifying the Lord when we are actually glorifying ourselves?*

....

....

....

....

3. *How are you inclined to be self-centered rather than God-centered in the ways you use your time? Confess these areas to the Lord in prayer.*

....

....

....

....

....

....

....

....

PART TWO

Priorities

Day 6   Why the Right Priorities Matter

Day 7   God

Day 8   Family

Day 9   Church & Christian Fellowship

Day 10   Work

Day 11   Service

Day 12   Stewardship

Day 13   Self-Care

Why the Right Priorities Matter

Take a moment to consider what makes up most of your time. Is it work? Household tasks? Taking care of little ones? A priority is something we believe is important, and what takes up most of our time reveals our priorities. What makes setting intentional priorities tricky is that, more than we realize, we can easily prioritize something that is not necessary or healthy. For example, we might prioritize watching television over exercising. Or we might prioritize playing golf on the weekends over spending time with family. These things are not in and of themselves bad things, but they can sometimes reveal how certain priorities are not always right.

What are the right priorities, then? While right priorities can be seen as subjective, as followers of Christ, our priorities should be birthed out of our worship of God. As we have discussed, our worship of God should be central to our lives. However, when our worship shifts from God to ourselves, our priorities will often shift and become focused on what makes us feel good or happy. As believers, we are to care more about our holiness than our momentary happiness. While joy is a part of the Christian life, God commands us to be holy as He is holy (1 Peter 1:16). Our holiness as believers should be our goal, and we pursue holiness by making our worship of God our ultimate priority. And it is our obedience to the command to be holy that leads us to the true joy that is found in Christ alone. When worshiping God is our ultimate priority, all our other priorities are put in their proper place.

In order to keep worship to God central, we must regularly meditate on the gospel. The more our hearts reflect on the gospel, the more our hearts respond to God in worship. In fact, continuously meditating on the gospel motivates us to establish priorities that form us in our holiness. We respond to what Christ has done for us by serving Him with joy and seeking to grow in our relationship with Him. As we aim to serve the Lord and grow in holiness, our priorities will be worship-oriented and gospel-centered.

In this section, we will discuss important priorities we should have as followers of Christ. While these priorities are not exhaustive, they make up biblical principles and teachings we should aim to apply in our lives. It is important to know that we cannot balance all of our priorities perfectly. No matter how hard we try, we cannot give equal attention and effort to every worship-oriented, gospel-centered priority. But that does not mean we should not seek to make these things a regular priority.

As you go through this section, take some time to evaluate what you are making a priority in your life. Ask the Lord to reveal if you are prioritizing other things that are not born from worship to God and a desire for holiness. And with the grace of Christ and the power of the Spirit, seek to prioritize what truly matters.

When worshiping God is our ultimate priority, all our other priorities are put in their proper place.

1. Read Matthew 6:33. What does it practically look like to seek first the kingdom of God and His righteousness? How does Matthew 6:33 teach us what we should prioritize?

....

....

....

....

2. Why is it important to evaluate our priorities?

....

....

....

....

3. List out your main priorities below.

....

....

....

....

....

....

....

....

God

When God rescued the Israelites from slavery, He knew that the Israelites had just left a nation that worshiped other gods. Not only this, but He knew they were also journeying to a land full of pagans who worshiped false gods as well. Because of this reality, God told the Israelites, "I am the Lord your God, who brought you out of the land of Egypt, out of the place of slavery. Do not have other gods besides me" (Exodus 20:2–3). He also instructed them to "love the Lord your God with all your heart, with all your soul, and with all your strength" (Deuteronomy 6:5). The Israelites' obedience to God would flow from their worship of Him and their love for Him. God was to be Israel's number one priority, and they were to seek Him first, follow His commands, and worship Him with all of who they were. The same is true for believers today. As followers of Christ, God is to be first in our lives.

Love for God and worship of Him should be what matters most to us. Why? Because God is the One who created us, and He created us to worship Him alone. We were made for God, and He is to be the object of our sole devotion. However, sin keeps us from worshiping God as we should. It encourages us to worship ourselves or other things of this world that make us feel happy. But this is why God gave us Jesus. Through the sacrifice of Christ on the cross, we are brought into a relationship with God and given the ability to worship Him as we should.

Yet we can still put other things before the Lord. When we become too busy, we can allow other things, even good things, to become the top priority in our lives. When God is not our number one priority, we will try to fit God into our lives rather than orienting our lives around Him. We must remember that Christ died so that God could be first in our lives. Without the grace of Christ, we have no ability of our own to make our relationship with God our main priority. But the grace of Jesus, given to us through His sacrifice, enables us to put God first.

Putting God first involves us regularly being in prayer and Bible study. It looks like choosing to do what is pleasing to the Lord rather than what is pleasing to ourselves. Putting God first also means making our primary motivation obedience and worship to the Lord. As we have discussed, putting God first will often be difficult and must be intentional, but when we remember the gospel and the grace Jesus has given us, we will be humbled. This humility will cause us, with the help of the Spirit, to remove or shift what is keeping God from being first in our lives. Though our hearts may struggle to prioritize our relationship with God, let us aim to worship God with all of who we are.

LOVE FOR GOD AND WORSHIP OF HIM SHOULD BE WHAT MATTERS MOST TO US.

The grace of Jesus, given to us through His sacrifice, enables us to put God first.

1. *Why should your relationship with God be a priority?*

....

....

....

....

2. *How have you seen the negative effects of failing to make God a priority?*

....

....

....

....

3. *Take a moment to consider how you can make God a priority in your daily life. Below, list out three ways you can put this into practice.*

....

....

....

....

....

....

....

....

Family

Scripture shows us the importance of worshiping God above everything. However, it also reveals the significance and value of family (Psalm 127:3, Matthew 15:4). God made the first family in the garden of Eden because He did not create man to be alone (Genesis 2:18–23). God commanded this family, Adam and Eve, to be fruitful and multiply and rule the earth under God's sovereignty (Genesis 1:28). Through obeying this command, God's glory would spread as their family flourished. The same is true for families today. The true purpose of family is to bring God glory and spread His glory through flourishing and obedience to Him.

Unfortunately, in many cultures, the significance of family has waned over the years. While many countries still value family, the individualism of other cultures has caused family to take the back seat. Adult children may neglect the care of their elderly parents. Parents with taxing jobs may put their work above their children. The busyness of life can make us become so focused on ourselves that we can go weeks without seeing or talking to our family.

It is also possible for us to believe we are making family a priority when in reality, we are not. Our schedules may involve our family, but that does not mean we are being intentional with our family by helping them grow and thrive. For example, if a family goes on vacation but a parent spends all of their time on the phone with work, that parent is neglecting the time they should be sharing with their family. In the same way, we can place other priorities before our families without even realizing it.

Family is a gift, and we should treasure this gift God gave us. Even if we do not have a family in the traditional sense, that does not mean we should neglect those God has placed in our lives who act as our family. Although relationships within our families can be messy, we should prioritize giving God glory in the ways we love and care for our family. This means that we will have to make sacrifices in order to make family a priority. We will have to say no to certain opportunities or work requests to make it to our daughter's piano recital, our son's baseball game, or our sister's art show. We will need to put the laptop or phone away to spend intentional time with our spouses when the work day is done. And we will have to set aside time, even if it is time off, to visit and see our parents or siblings.

Though making sacrifices for our family can be difficult, the time we spend with our family is precious, and the ways in which we invest in our family cultivate worship of God. When we prioritize family as believers, we point the world to the love of our heavenly Father, who invites us into His family, giving God the glory He so deserves.

> " FAMILY IS A GIFT, AND WE SHOULD TREASURE THIS GIFT GOD GAVE US.

The ways in which we invest in our family cultivate worship of God.

1. *Why is family important? Why have many societies diminished the importance of family or changed what family represents?*

....

....

....

....

2. *Besides the Lord, what do you prioritize above your family?*

....

....

....

....

3. *What are some practical ways you can prioritize your family?*
   List three ways below.

....

....

....

....

....

....

....

Church &
Christian Fellowship

It is Sunday morning, and your alarm goes off.
You look at your phone and debate getting up. If
you get up now, you will have enough time to get
yourself together and make it to church. But if
you snooze, you will miss church and have more
time to sleep. What do you choose?

We all have moments when our consistency in
church participation wavers. There are some
Sundays when we or our family members are
sick. There are times when we are out of town
and do not have the opportunity to make it to
church. But there are also situations in which we
consciously choose to do something in the place
of church. We decide to go to the beach or eat out
for breakfast. Or we choose to sleep in because
we had a busy week.

The Church is vital to our spiritual health as
believers (Hebrews 10:24–25). To not value the
Church and participate in the Church is to keep
ourselves from the source of our spiritual forma-
tion. We might think we can do the Christian
life on our own without the Church, but we
cannot. While there are personal aspects to our
relationship with God, such as individual time
in God's Word and prayer, believers are also to
be a corporate people. Coming together as God's
people, the Church, shapes us in our holiness.

When Jesus went to the cross, He died so that all of those who believed in Him would be one as God's people (John 17). It is the grace of Christ that unites us as God's people, and when we gather together as believers, we share that grace with one another. We sing songs, praising God for who He is and what He has done for us through Christ. We listen to the Word of God that reminds us of the beauty of the gospel. The Church is a gift that allows us to marvel and respond to the amazing grace of Christ together.

But we miss out on experiencing this gift of grace when we do not consistently attend church on Sundays or gather together for Christian fellowship during the week. Allowing ourselves to be too busy for church hurts us in our holiness. When we try to live our lives with little-to-no church attendance or fellowship, we become more formed by the world than by God's Word. If we are not regularly sitting under the Word of God, discussing the truth of God's Word with others, and confessing our sins with other believers, we will instead be shaped by what the world values and preaches.

Unless an extenuating circumstance arises, we should prioritize regular church attendance and fellowship. Making the Church and fellowship with believers a priority will require us to make sacrifices, but these sacrifices are always worthwhile. When church and Christian fellowship are a priority, our worship is strengthened, our faith is deepened, and God is glorified.

Coming together as God's people, the Church, shapes us in our holiness.

1. *Why is it important to prioritize church and Christian fellowship?*

....

....

....

....

2. *What are some sacrifices you will have to make in order to make the Church and Christian fellowship a priority?*

....

....

....

....

3. *What are some practical ways you can prioritize the Church and fellowship with other believers? List out three ways below.*

....

....

....

....

....

....

....

....

Work

Work can be a tricky priority because it is possible to allow our work to keep us from working toward other priorities. Nevertheless, work is important, and when we view our work rightly, we labor hard while also making time for what matters. But what is work? Sometimes, work can be seen as only a nine-to-five job or paid position, but as believers, work is anything we do with our hands to bring glory to God. For instance, parenting, volunteering, building, and creating are all wonderful examples of work.

We receive a vision of what work was designed to be in the garden of Eden. Genesis 2:15 tells us how Adam was placed in the garden to work and watch over the ground. This idea around work appears again in Numbers 3:7 to describe the priests' work for God in the temple. Therefore, work is worship. As Adam cultivated the creation around him, he brought glory to God. Work was a delight in the garden because it caused Adam and Eve to enjoy the fruits of their labor while also joyfully praising God.

However, the Fall complicated work. We read in Genesis 3:17–19 how joyful work was traded for burdensome work as a consequence of sin. Now, all humanity has to toil in order to provide for and sustain ourselves and our families. But Jesus restores and redeems our work because, through Christ, our work has eternal purposes. Believers' work is different from the work of those who do not know God because God uses our work for His kingdom. While work can still be hard and tiring, believers can labor with joy, knowing their labor in the Lord is not in vain (Colossians 3:23–24).

The truth that our work matters should cause us to prioritize work. At times, laziness can settle in because we forget or push down the reality that our labor is purposeful. When we are tempted to be lazy, we must remember that we work for a greater purpose. We are a part of God's kingdom and have the opportunity to work for His glory here on earth. However, we should be careful not to prioritize our work for the wrong reasons. It is possible for us to prioritize our work so that we can be impressive in the eyes of others or compete with others. When work becomes more about us and our glory rather than God's, we lose sight of the purpose of our labor. And when we lose sight of this purpose, we can allow work to take the place of other priorities, such as time with God, our families, and Christian community.

When God's glory is at the center of our work, we will labor with the right intentions. We will seek to work hard for the Lord while also prioritizing the rest of what God's Word teaches. So let us work heartily for God's glory and remember to lay our work down so that we can pick up what God has asked of us.

> JESUS RESTORES AND REDEEMS OUR WORK BECAUSE, THROUGH CHRIST, OUR WORK HAS ETERNAL PURPOSES.

When God's glory is at the center of our work, we will labor with the right intentions.

1. *How has God called you to work in this season?*

....

....

....

....

2. *How does the truth that your work matters to God and His kingdom motivate you to prioritize work?*

....

....

....

....

3. *How can you prioritize work without being kept from other important priorities? List three ways below.*

....

....

....

....

....

....

....

....

....

DAY II

Service

What comes into your mind when you think of the word "service"? Perhaps you think of someone in the military who serves their country by protecting it from attack. Or maybe you think of someone in the service industry who waits tables and brings people the meals they have ordered. We may admire those who serve others while forgetting that, as believers, we are called to serve others as well. However, we may feel too busy to serve others, especially if we feel like all of our time is spent taking care of our kids or working at our jobs. Even still, God's Word encourages us to make service a priority.

Galatians 5:13–14 says, "For you were called to be free, brothers and sisters; only don't use this freedom as an opportunity for the flesh, but serve one another through love. For the whole law is fulfilled in one statement: Love your neighbor as yourself." Paul teaches us in these verses how the grace of Christ gives us freedom from sin. Yet, we are not to take Christ's forgiveness as a license to do what we please, especially by serving our own interests. Instead, we are to obey the command to love our neighbor as ourselves through our service to others.

If we took a look at our schedules, we might find that we are doing more to serve ourselves than others. We might see areas where we fill our time with what makes us feel good and happy. And while it is not wrong to do things that bring us joy, our schedules should not be made up of what only benefits us. Even if we feel as if time is limited due to our work and roles, we can make sacrifices in our schedules for the sake of others.

When we make sacrifices to serve others, we reflect Jesus, who "did not come to be served, but to serve, and to give his life as a ransom for many" (Mark 10:45). The sacrificial service of Christ on the cross motivates us to serve others willingly and joyfully. And in the moments we find ourselves struggling to desire to serve, we can remember the sacrifice of Christ and the lengths He took so we could receive salvation.

So, how can we prioritize service? Prioritizing regular service might look like serving at your church a few Sundays a month. It could look like volunteering at a local shelter every other week or once a month. Or it could be simply making yourself available to help friends when needs arise and adjusting your schedule to meet those needs. There are many ways we can make service a priority in our lives if we take the time to think through potential opportunities and make an effort to take up those opportunities. As followers of Christ, we are called to be servants of God and others, so may we make it a priority as we take up this call with joy.

> WE CAN MAKE SACRIFICES IN OUR SCHEDULES FOR THE SAKE OF OTHERS.

As followers of Christ, we are called to be servants of God and others.

1. *Why is service important as followers of Christ?*

....

....

....

....

2. *What keeps you from making service a priority?*

....

....

....

....

3. *What are some practical ways you can prioritize serving others?*
    List out three ways below.

....

....

....

....

....

....

....

....

Stewardship

Think about your favorite item. What would you do if someone took that item and completely ruined it? You would probably be upset or angry. Your response would make sense because that person would have failed to take care of something you hold dear. The truth is, each one of us mishandles God's gifts. Everything we have is a gift from God, yet we can often disregard or forget this truth. When we are too busy, we can neglect taking care of what God has given us. Tomorrow, we will discuss the importance of stewarding our bodies, specifically, but God calls us to steward every one of His gifts, no matter how busy we are.

One area in which we can prioritize stewardship is by stewarding our finances. Regardless of the amount of money in our accounts, the Bible commands us to steward our finances wisely. Proverbs 3:9 tells us to "honor the Lord with your wealth, with the firstfruits of all your crops" (NIV). We honor the Lord with our wealth by spending our money wisely and by viewing what we have ultimately as the Lord's. Yet, when life gets busy, we might not steward our money well. We may make rash financial decisions without thinking things through because we feel rushed. Or we might not take the time to create and cultivate a budget for wise spending. When we prioritize stewardship of our finances, we slow down and consider the ways we should handle our money for God's glory.

Another area in which we can prioritize stewardship is by stewarding creation. Creation is a gift from God, but like a person who ruins our favorite item, we, too, can ruin God's creation as we fail to take care of the nature around us. Busyness causes us to believe that we do not have time to steward God's creation, but not doing so rejects God's command to rule and subdue the earth with wisdom and intentionality (Genesis 1:28).

Lastly, we can prioritize stewardship by managing the seemingly ordinary items in our care. If all that we have is God's and a gift from Him, we should handle what He gives us mindfully. This means that we should not push off cleaning our homes, maintaining our vehicles, or keeping our pets healthy to the best of our ability. When we do not prioritize stewarding these gifts well, we essentially belittle the good gifts God has given us. While we cannot be perfect stewards in all areas of our lives, we can still seek to respond to God's good gifts with care and consideration. This might look like taking a night out of the month to go over your finances, spending Saturday morning to cultivate a garden, or setting aside five to ten minutes of your day to tidy up around your house. We are not too busy to steward God's gifts, so let us take care of what God has graciously bestowed upon us.

> GOD CALLS US TO STEWARD EVERY ONE OF HIS GIFTS, NO MATTER HOW BUSY WE ARE.

God blessed them,
and God said to
them, "Be fruitful,
multiply, fill the
earth, and subdue
it. Rule the fish of
the sea, the birds
of the sky, and
every creature that
crawls on the earth."

GENESIS 1:28

1. *What does it mean to be a good steward?*

....

....

....

....

2. *How does busyness prevent you from stewardship?*

....

....

....

....

3. *What are some practical ways you can prioritize stewardship?*
    List three ways below.

....

....

....

....

....

....

....

....

....

Self-Care

In the busyness of life, care for ourselves can fall by the wayside. A jam-packed schedule can keep us from regular checkups at the doctor. We can be so fixated on doing what needs to get done that we forget to eat or drink water. We can push down the warning signs our bodies give us, such as regular sleepless nights, headaches, or constant stress. While self-care can be applied wrongly—for example, by seeing meaningless activities as the means for self-care or by believing wholeness and happiness lie within—it is biblical to take care of our bodies.

One of the greatest biblical principles pertaining to self-care is rest. While we will discuss rest in more depth later on in this booklet, it is important to consider rest when thinking about self-care. God created us to need rest, and He even commanded rest as a regular discipline for His people (Exodus 20:8). Even though the Sabbath rest we see in Scripture is ultimately fulfilled in Christ (Matthew 11:28, 12:8), it is important for us as believers to take up the gift of rest. God did not make us to be like machines, always going and never stopping. In order to take care of ourselves and do our work effectively, we need to rest.

Self-care involves our bodies, but it also involves our minds. Mental health is important, but constantly being on the go can cause us to neglect our mental health. When we move from one thing to the next, we do not always allow ourselves the time we need to process our thoughts and emotions. If something happens that triggers an insecurity or makes us anxious, we can suppress these thoughts and feelings. But like boiling water that overflows on a hot stove, the more we suppress our emotions, the more our emotions can build up until we explode. It is important that we take the time to process what we are feeling, even though doing so can be difficult. Rather than pushing everything down, we can share our fears and frustrations with a trusted friend or counselor and take our cares to the Lord through prayer.

We will not be able to do what God calls us to do well if we do not take care of ourselves. Our relationships with others will suffer if we are too stressed to have a conversation. Our work will suffer if we are too tired or burned out to focus. And ultimately, the longevity of our health will suffer if we do not prioritize our health in the present the best we are able. While our schedules should not revolve around us, it is not wrong to set aside or plan times to exercise, rest, and de-stress. Self-care with the right motivation is not only healthy—it is holy. As we care for our bodies and depend on the Lord, we steward the bodies God has given us well, glorifying the Lord as we do so.

" IT IS BIBLICAL TO TAKE CARE OF OUR BODIES.

As we care for our bodies and depend on the Lord, we steward the bodies God has given us well.

1. *Why is it important to view self-care with the right perspective as believers?*

....

....

....

....

2. *In what ways do you neglect self-care due to busyness?*

....

....

....

....

3. *How can you practically prioritize self-care? List out three ways you can put self-care into practice.*

....

....

....

....

....

....

....

....

....

PART THREE

Making a Plan

Day 14   Evaluating Our Time

Day 15   Setting Goals

Day 16   Establishing Boundaries

Day 17   Pursuing Accountability

Day 18   Putting It All Together

Evaluating Our Time

We have discussed the problem of busyness and considered the priorities we should have as believers. While you have been evaluating your time as you have gone through the previous sections, it is time to evaluate your time more critically and make a plan to live fruitfully and faithfully rather than constantly feeling frazzled. Before we dive into what today's reading entails, take a moment to breathe and remember the purpose of this thirty-day challenge. This challenge is not meant to make you feel ashamed and guilty for how you use your time. This challenge is not meant to overwhelm your already busy life. This challenge is meant to help you love and glorify God by living wisely and intentionally. Remember to approach this part of the challenge not with a mentality to earn God's favor through your time but with the mentality to further worship the Lord with your time because of the favor that is already yours in Christ.

In preparation for making a plan, you will list out how you use your time and evaluate what you do with your time. On the next page, you will find a chart that allows you to fill in what a typical week looks like for you. You may consider pausing progress in this booklet and filling out this chart as you go through an actual week. Or, you can simply think through your typical week and fill the chart out that way. After filling out this chart, you will answer some questions to help you evaluate your week.

Before you begin evaluating your time, open your Bible to Psalm 90. Take a moment to read through this Psalm and meditate on its words. Once you have finished reading, pray the prayer below, and begin the chart.

God, You are an eternal God. You are from eternity to eternity. Yet I am not like You. While You have given me eternal life through Your Son, my life is a vapor. My days here on earth are limited. Therefore, teach me to number my days. Teach me to not allow my days to pass by quickly without thinking critically about how I should use my time wisely. Keep me from being so busy that I do not take the life You have given me seriously. Thank You, Lord, for Your faithful love and for giving me Your grace through Jesus. May Your faithful love and grace encourage me to glorify You with my time. Expose the areas of my life where busyness is keeping me from living faithfully for You, and establish the work of my hands for Your glory. Amen.

" THIS CHALLENGE IS MEANT TO HELP YOU LOVE AND GLORIFY GOD BY LIVING WISELY AND INTENTIONALLY.

	SUNDAY	MONDAY	TUESDAY
6:00 AM			
6:30 AM			
7:00 AM			
7:30 AM			
8:00 AM			
8:30 AM			
9:00 AM			
9:30 AM			
10:00 AM			
10:30 AM			
11:00 AM			
11:30 AM			
12:00 PM			
12:30 PM			
1:00 PM			
1:30 PM			
2:00 PM			
2:30 PM			
3:00 PM			
3:30 PM			
4:00 PM			
4:30 PM			
5:00 PM			
5:30 PM			
6:00 PM			
6:30 PM			
7:00 PM			
7:30 PM			
8:00 PM			
8:30 PM			
9:00 PM			
9:30 PM			
10:00 PM			
10:30 PM			

WEDNESDAY	THURSDAY	FRIDAY	SATURDAY

Lord, you have been our refuge in every generation. Before the mountains were born, before you gave birth to the earth and the world, from eternity to eternity, you are God.

PSALM 90:1–2

1. *What are the things in your week that are important to keep?*

....

....

....

....

....

2. *In what ways do you see yourself using your time well in your typical week? How can you keep this up? On the other hand, in what ways do you see yourself not using your time well in your typical week?*

....

....

....

....

....

3. *What are some things that are not necessary and contributing to your busyness that you can remove or change?*

....

....

....

....

....

Setting Goals

When a new year begins, we can be filled with motivation and excitement to plan and implement goals. With a fresh new year in front of us, we can feel as if anything is possible—as if now is the time to do what we have been pushing off, to do what we felt scared to do the year before. However, as the year progresses, we might find the initial thrill fading. Maybe we have made some progress with our goals, but now we feel our discipline waning and our drive disappearing. Or perhaps our schedules have become so full that we believe we do not have the time to reach the goals we initially set for ourselves.

While keeping track of and accomplishing goals can be difficult, setting goals for ourselves helps us grow and stay on top of what is important. Yesterday, you took time to examine your week and evaluate how you use your time. After answering yesterday's questions, you should have an idea of what you should eliminate from your schedule and what you should keep. But actually sticking to this ideal schedule and lifestyle can be challenging. This is why the next step is to set personal goals. These goals are designed to keep you from chronic busyness and help you dedicate your time to what matters.

To make your goals more achievable, you will break your goals into monthly, weekly, and daily goals. This will help you make progress toward your goals over time, which helps keep your motivation strong. You will find some charts on the next page where you can set and plan out your goals. In thinking about the goals you want to achieve, take a moment to reflect on the priorities we covered in the last section and your answers for how you can prioritize those priorities. Then, consider what goals you can make based on those priorities. For example, one of the priorities we discussed is self-care. One goal you might set for yourself is to exercise regularly. A breakdown of that goal might look like this:

MONTHLY GOAL:
Exercise three to four times a week.

WEEKLY GOAL:
Go for a run once and do an at-home workout twice a week.

DAILY GOAL:
Accomplish at least fifteen to twenty minutes of physical activity a day.

In the monthly goals section, write out three to five big-picture goals for the month. Then, come up with three to five weekly goals that will aid you in reaching your designated monthly goals, and place those in the weekly goal section. Lastly, establish three to five daily goals based on your monthly and weekly goals, and place those in the daily goals section. Each of these three sections includes boxes for you to check off your progress. It is okay if you do not check off these boxes perfectly. Growth is not about perfection but progression, so rejoice if progress is made, and rest in Christ's grace and strength to keep trying if your progress falters.

MONTHLY GOALS

DAILY GOALS

	1	2	3	4	5	6	7	8	9	10	11	12

WEEKLY GOALS

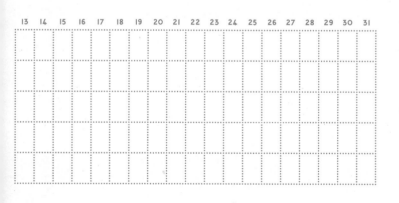

Establishing Boundaries

As you prepare to make a plan, it is important to consider boundaries. One of the reasons we can become too busy is that we do not set boundaries. Think of a boundary as something that protects your time. Without boundaries, it is possible to say yes to things you should not say yes to or use your time to do something that takes away from something else that is more important. When you set boundaries, you essentially establish a limit. You commit yourself to do what you have put inside that boundary, but anything that will push you outside of that boundary is off-limits.

An example of a boundary could be that you do not take any work calls or respond to any work emails once you return home for the day. Another boundary could be that you reserve every Friday evening for time with your family. While emergencies or other unforeseen circumstances can certainly disrupt boundaries, the only other real disruption for your boundaries is yourself. If you do not set, maintain, and protect boundaries, you can allow yourself to perpetuate unhealthy habits of busyness.

While it can be easy to establish boundaries, protecting them can be hard. We may feel guilty for declining an invitation so that we can rest or waiting to respond to someone until the morning so that we can focus on dinner with our kids. At other times, we will fail to maintain a boundary and go over that designated line. God's Word meets us in both of these moments by reminding us that we were not made to please man but to honor the Lord (Galatians 1:10). So even though we may feel a twinge of guilt when we refuse to do something to maintain a boundary, we can be comforted by remembering that we honor the Lord when we protect what matters to Him.

God's Word meets us in the moments we fail by reminding us that we have God's grace through Christ (2 Corinthians 12:9). Although we can fail to use our time wisely by pushing beyond boundaries, we have God's forgiveness for our failures in Christ. God's grace does not permit us to continue making mistakes. Rather, God's grace encourages us to keep seeking faithfulness to the Lord as we walk in His grace and forgiveness.

In order to set boundaries, you must establish your priorities and define your limits. Based on the content and your answers in this booklet so far, what is the most important to you? What do you need to focus on the most in your daily life? What keeps you from those priorities? What leaves you feeling overwhelmed and exhausted? Answering these questions will help you see what you want to focus your attention on most in your life. They will also help you evaluate what you need to say no to so that those priorities are protected. So take a moment to consider and reflect on those questions on pages 76–77.

REFLECT

1. What are my priorities?

....

....

....

....

....

....

2. What keeps me from these priorities?

....

....

....

....

....

....

3. What leaves me overwhelmed and exhausted?

....

....

....

....

....

....

After answering these questions, spend some time brainstorming what boundaries you can establish with your priorities. For example:

> **PRIORITY:** Attend church every Sunday.
>
> **BOUNDARIES:** Come home early from events or gatherings on Saturdays in order to get to sleep at a reasonable time. Don't make plans with others when church meets unless it's necessary.

Priority:

Boundaries:

Priority:

Boundaries:

Priority:

Boundaries:

Priority:

Boundaries:

Priority:

Boundaries:

Pursuing Accountability

When it comes to trying to move away from living lives that are too busy, we need the help of other people. We need others to give us not only support and encouragement but also accountability. Without accountability, it can be easy to break our boundaries. It can be easy to make excuses for unhealthy habits or be completely unaware that we are taking on too much. So, as you make your plan, consider who can hold you accountable. This person might be someone who you see daily or regularly, like a spouse, parent, or co-worker—someone who naturally observes your life and can speak into your life when they notice you perpetuating busyness. This could look like this person intentionally checking in with you regularly. For example, you could ask a good friend to text you during the week and ask how your goals are going.

Once you choose a person who can hold you account-able, ask that person if they are willing to do so. Come up with a plan for what that accountability might look like. While your accountability partner is there to speak into your life, it can also be helpful to ask your partner questions as you work toward minimizing busyness. Some potential questions might include: *Do you see any areas of my life where I am too busy? In what ways do you see me prioritizing _____ in this season?*

Choosing accountability is one thing, but listening to accountability is another thing. At times, we may find our flesh opposing the accountability of another.

We might feel frustrated when someone lovingly corrects us, or we might brush off someone's words of wisdom. Because of this, it's important to keep two truths in mind as you rely on accountability.

1. Accountability is for your good.

Proverbs 27:17 tells us, "Iron sharpens iron, and one person sharpens another." Just as knives need to be sharpened to be effective, so do we need to be sharpened in order to grow and live faithfully. While receiving the correction that comes with accountability can be difficult, even painful at times, it is for your good. Receive accountability with gratitude, knowing that it is shaping and helping you.

2. The Holy Spirit helps you receive accountability.

Even if we acknowledge that accountability is for our good, we might still find ourselves rejecting counsel and correction. Thankfully, God gives believers the Holy Spirit to help them in the areas where they are weak. It is only by the Holy Spirit's power that we can remove pride, humbly listen, and receive accountability. When you find your flesh seeking to shut down accountability, ask the Spirit to help you receive accountability willingly and joyfully.

As you remember the gift of accountability and the Spirit's help in accountability, you will both desire and receive the accountability of others. You were not made to do this life alone, so take up the gift of accountability and allow others to help you.

You were not made to do this life alone.

1. *Why is accountability important?*

....

....

....

....

....

....

2. *Who can hold you accountable for how you spend your time?*

....

....

....

....

....

3. *What would this accountability look like?*

....

....

....

....

....

DAY 18

Putting It All Together

You have evaluated your time, set goals, established boundaries, and pursued accountability. Now, it is time to put it all together. Following this day, you will find some pages that you will fill out over the course of four weeks. These pages will help you keep track of how you are using your time and allow you to evaluate whether you are using time wisely and faithfully unto the Lord as the days progress. Start these pages today, and continue them as you begin part four. It is up to you if you want to keep working through them after you conclude this booklet or if you want to work through them all before starting part five. Remember to rely on the Lord as you go through these pages, asking for and depending on His strength to help you be faithful with your time. The following verses are to encourage you as you begin. Read these verses slowly, and reflect on the God who is with you and who goes before you!

PSALM 16:5–8

Lord, you are my portion and my cup of blessing; you hold my future. The boundary lines have fallen for me in pleasant places; indeed, I have a beautiful inheritance. I will bless the Lord who counsels me—even at night when my thoughts trouble me. I always let the Lord guide me. Because he is at my right hand, I will not be shaken.

PSALM 143:8-10

Let me experience your faithful love in the morning, for I trust in you. Reveal to me the way I should go because I appeal to you. Rescue me from my enemies, Lord; I come to you for protection. Teach me to do your will, for you are my God. May your gracious Spirit lead me on level ground.

LUKE 10:38-42

While they were traveling, he entered a village, and a woman named Martha welcomed him into her home. She had a sister named Mary, who also sat at the Lord's feet and was listening to what he said. But Martha was distracted by her many tasks, and she came up and asked, "Lord, don't you care that my sister has left me to serve alone? So tell her to give me a hand." The Lord answered her, "Martha, Martha, you are worried and upset about many things, but one thing is necessary. Mary has made the right choice, and it will not be taken away from her."

"

REMEMBER TO RELY ON THE LORD
AS YOU GO THROUGH THESE PAGES,
ASKING FOR AND DEPENDING
ON HIS STRENGTH.

NOTES

How I Used My Time Today

Monday ....

....

Tuesday ....

....

Wednesday ....

....

Thursday ....

....

Friday ....

....

Saturday ....

....

Sunday ....

....

1. *How did I use my time well this week?*

....

....

2. *What do I need to do next week so that I continue to use my time wisely?*

....

....

How I Used My Time Today

Monday ....

....

Tuesday ....

....

Wednesday ....

....

Thursday ....

....

Friday ....

....

Saturday ....

....

Sunday ....

....

1. *How did I use my time well this week?*

....

....

2. *What do I need to do next week so that I continue to use my time wisely?*

....

....

How I Used My Time Today

Monday ....

....

Tuesday ....

....

Wednesday ....

....

Thursday ....

....

Friday ....

....

Saturday ....

....

Sunday ....

....

1. How did I use my time well this week?

....

....

2. What do I need to do next week so that I continue to use my time wisely?

....

....

How I Used My Time Today

Monday ....

....

Tuesday ....

....

Wednesday ....

....

Thursday ....

....

Friday ....

....

Saturday ....

....

Sunday ....

....

1. *How did I use my time well this week?*

....

....

2. *What do I need to do next week so that I continue to use my time wisely?*

....

....

PART FOUR

Truth to Remember

Day 19 You Are Not Limitless

Day 20 You Are Not in Control

Day 21 You Are Not Omnipresent

Day 22 The Importance of Rest

Day 23 The Importance of Stillness

Day 24 The Importance of Prayer

Day 25 The Importance of Bible Study

Day 26 It's Okay to Say "No"

Day 27 It's Okay to Slow Down

Day 28 It's Okay to Ask for Help

You Are Not Limitless

Perhaps one of the most frustrating qualities of being human is having limits. At some point in the day, we all grow tired. We can exert strength for a while, but at some point, we get weak. We might be able to focus and work diligently for an extended period of time, but at some point, our brain grows heavy, and our concentration wanes. These limits can cause us to wish that we were like the superheroes we watch in movies who have unlimited strength and abilities. Unfortunately, we are not superheroes. But the problem is that we often act as if we were unlimited. We can push down the reality of our limits by packing as much into our schedules as possible. Or we can ignore our limits and try to keep going without stopping, perpetuating burnout and fatigue. While limits can be frustrating, it is good to acknowledge our limits. Admitting our limits enables us to go to God, who has no limits, and place our trust in Him.

Isaiah 40:28–31 tells us:

> *Do you not know? Have you not heard? The Lord is the everlasting God, the Creator of the whole earth. He never becomes faint or weary; there is no limit to his understanding. He gives strength to the faint and strengthens the powerless. Youths may become faint and weary, and young men stumble and fall, but those who trust*

in the Lord will renew their strength; they will
soar on wings like eagles; they will run and not
become weary, they will walk and not faint.

When we read these verses, it is possible to zero in on the part that says we will run without growing weary and walk without growing faint when we receive God's strength. These verses might make us believe that receiving God's strength makes us limitless. However, Isaiah 40:28–31 is meant to encourage us to seek God's strength rather than try to be strong in our own power. The passage teaches us that God's strength enables us to persevere and handle what we could not in our strength alone. But it does not affirm that God makes us limitless. Rather, those who trust in the God who has no limits will find themselves continuously strengthened by Him.

Instead of seeking to push beyond our limits, we must look to God, who has none. When we look to the Lord, we are reminded that only God is limitless, that only God can never grow weary and never run out of strength. So, rather than trying to be like God, let us surrender the truth that we are not. When we admit our limits, we are kept from trying to fit as much as we can into our schedule. Instead of burning out, we are able to slow down and create boundaries with our time. So instead of rejecting your limits, allow your limits to reveal your need for God and His strength. You are not limitless, and that is a good thing.

Admitting our limits enables us to go to God, who has no limits, and place our trust in Him.

1. *In what ways do you try to be limitless?*

....

....

....

....

....

....

2. *How does trying to be limitless perpetuate busyness in your life?*

....

....

....

....

....

3. *How can reminding yourself of who God is and your need for His strength keep you from trying to be limitless?*

....

....

....

....

....

You Are Not in Control

Though a car has many parts that all work together to form the car and make it operate, it is the steering wheel that ultimately controls the vehicle. In our own lives, we can metaphorically try to take the steering wheel, aiming to control every area of our lives. While we can believe that we are the ones who ultimately control our lives, God is in control. He is the One who controls all things, including our lives. Though God gives us the freedom to make decisions, He is the One who ultimately works in and through us. Proverbs 19:21 explains this truth: "Many plans are in a person's heart, but the Lord's decree will prevail." He is the One who establishes His plans for us, no matter how much we try to make plans ourselves.

But even though we know God is in control, we can still try to grab the steering wheel. We can still try to do all we can to control our plans and the outcome of our situations. This need for control can perpetuate busyness in our lives. When we try to push down the truth that we are not in control, we can work ourselves into a frenzy. We can try to hold together all the pieces of our lives in our own power, even though we were never meant to do so. And when we are unable to hold all these pieces together and they fall apart, we can become overwhelmed.

When our perfectly planned-out day is ruined or when something we did not see coming messes up our week, we receive a rude awakening that we are not in control. Just as admitting our limits is for our good, so is admitting our lack of control for our good. Admitting our lack of control helps us to place control in God's hands and be still. When we take our hands off the steering wheel and give control to God, we can trust Him wherever He leads.

Releasing control is difficult, but this is why God gives us the Holy Spirit. As believers, we have the Holy Spirit who helps us trust God and release control to Him. The Holy Spirit convicts us when we are trying to control our lives and forge our own plans without considering the Lord. So in the moments we feel tempted to seize control of our lives and circumstances, we can ask for the Spirit's help. Daily asking for the Spirit to help us surrender control will also help us seek God's ways and plans over our own. As we seek to walk in God's ways and heed His plans, we will not grip tightly to our lives. Our days will start with open hands to God's will, rather than closed fists over our own. When we live this way, we will find peace in the place of panic and dependency in the place of distress.

> " ADMITTING OUR LACK OF CONTROL HELPS US TO PLACE CONTROL IN GOD'S HANDS AND BE STILL.

Many plans are in a person's heart, but the Lord's decree will prevail.

PROVERBS 19:21

1. *In what ways does the need for control perpetuate busyness in your life?*

....

....

....

....

....

2. *What is at the heart of your need for control?*

....

....

....

....

....

3. *What does it look like for you to practically surrender to God's control?*

....

....

....

....

....

You Are Not Omnipresent

If you have ever wanted to be in multiple places at once, the Four Corners is the place to go. The Four Corners is the quadripoint of four American states—Arizona, Colorado, New Mexico, and Utah—and this area allows you to stand in each of these four states at the same time. Though standing here is exciting, it is one of only a few places that allow you to be in more places than one. As humans, we are limited to location. We are not omnipresent, which means that we cannot be everywhere all at once. There is only One who can be omnipresent, and that is God. However, we can sometimes act as if we are omnipresent, even though we know we are not.

One of the primary ways we try to be omnipresent is by seeking to be all things for all people. We try to do as much as we can for others, always jumping at the opportunity to help others and always saying yes to requests. While the Bible does teach us to serve, care for, and help others, Scripture does not ask us to do everything for everyone all the time. Why? Because it is impossible for us to meet every need for every person. As we have already discussed, humans have limits, and one of these limits involves our availability. We can only do so much for others and be in so many places on any given day. But our packed schedules can often reveal our efforts to try to do everything for people and be everywhere we can. For example, we have probably all had days that look a little something like this: we meet with a struggling friend at 8:00, attend a board meeting at 9:00, give a ride to a neighbor during our lunch break at 11:00, attend a parent/teacher meeting at 5:00, watch our kid's dance recital at 6:30, serve dinner at youth group at 7:00, and pick up our other child from soccer practice at 8:00. While the specifics may look different for each person, it is normal to have days like this from time to time. But when our weeks are consistently this busy, it may reveal that we are trying to be omnipresent.

When we try to be omnipresent, we essentially try to be God. We try to do what only He can do, which is to be everywhere for everyone at all times. God did not create us to be omnipresent on purpose. Our inability to be all things for all people is meant to help us trust in the One who can. When we surrender our desire—and perhaps even our need—to be omnipresent, we trust God to work in the lives of others. We trust God to work in the places we cannot be. As we surrender our desire to be omnipresent, we are able to worship God for who He is rather than try to be like Him in the ways we are not. We are able to marvel at God's omnipresence, like David in Psalm 139. So, do what you can where you can, and allow God to take care of the rest, trusting Him to do what you cannot.

> " OUR INABILITY TO BE ALL THINGS FOR ALL PEOPLE IS MEANT TO HELP US TRUST IN THE ONE WHO CAN.

Do what you can where you can, and allow God to take care of the rest.

1. *Read Psalm 139:1–10. What do you learn about God's omnipresence in this passage?*

....

....

....

....

....

2. *In what ways do you try to be omnipresent?*

....

....

....

....

....

3. *How can reminding yourself that you are not omnipresent help you not take on too much?*

....

....

....

....

....

The Importance of Rest

On day 13, we briefly discussed how part of self-care involves giving ourselves rest. The theme of rest stretches all the way back to the beginning of creation. After God created the world, He rested (Genesis 2:1–2). This was not because He was tired. God rested because He finished all of His works of creation, and now He could celebrate this finished work. God's creation was essentially a place of rest because it was perfect. Without the presence of sin, the world was at peace, and God invited His creation to delight in this peace with Him. But when Adam and Eve sinned, they disrupted God's peace. The world was now a place of unrest, and Adam and Eve had to experience this unrest through hard work and suffering. Yet God had a plan to bring His creation back to a place of permanent rest.

As a foretaste of this rest, God established the Sabbath day and command (Exodus 20:8). After working six days, the Israelites were to rest on the Sabbath, the seventh day. The Israelites' dependence on God would be tested by their obedience to this command. Working on the Sabbath would reveal distrust in God's ability to provide. Our own refusal to rest can reveal the same distrust. We may know that God is our ultimate Provider, yet we can be afraid to stop striving, hurrying, or working ourselves to the bone. We can worry that if we allow ourselves to stop and rest, we might not be taken care of. So we keep going. We keep doing and doing so that we can hold our lives together. But the inevitable burnout we experience when we live this way reminds us that only God can hold our lives together. He is the One who ultimately takes care of us. When we stop and rest, we declare our dependence on God. We declare our trust in God to meet our needs.

The Sabbath command we read in the Old Testament ultimately points us to the rest we have in Christ. In Christ, we receive the forgiveness that gives us spiritual rest. But we should still physically rest as believers. Taking a weekly Sabbath or scheduling times to rest gives us a regular rhythm to stop and refresh. What we do with this rest is up to us, but it should involve us breaking from our regular work to relax. This rest could look like reading a good book, taking a walk, or spending extended time in Scripture. It could look like choosing not to do anything after work besides unwinding. When we take this time to rest, we will find ourselves much less hurried and stressed. We will be able to place our lives in God's hands and trust God to keep working even when we are not. So, if you find that rest is not a regular rhythm for you, seek to make it a rhythm. Rest is a gift that God gives you; take up that gift with joy and humility.

> " ONLY GOD CAN HOLD OUR LIVES TOGETHER.

When we stop and rest, we declare our dependence on God.

1. *What does rest look like in your life?*

....

....

....

....

....

....

2. *What is keeping you from experiencing rest?*

....

....

....

....

....

3. *How can you make rest a regular rhythm?*

....

....

....

....

....

The Importance of Stillness

When was the last time you had an extended moment to stop and be still? These moments can feel hard to come by in the busyness of our lives. Depending on how much is going on, we might be unable to remember the last time we took the time for stillness. The idea of being still may sound nice, but it might not feel possible due to our busy schedules. But stillness is important. Stillness allows us to stop the cycle of hurriedness. Stillness allows us to take a breath and calm our frantic minds and hearts. Yesterday, we discussed the importance of rest, and while stillness is related to rest, it is not the same as rest. Rest may involve stillness, but not every experience of rest has to do with being still. So what does it look like to be still?

During the Exodus through the Red Sea, the Israelites were being chased by Pharaoh's army. Though God was leading them, the Israelites cried out in fear in light of the army seeking to capture them or, worse, kill them. To encourage the Israelites, Moses told them, "Do not be afraid. Stand firm and you will see the deliverance the Lord will bring you today. The Egyptians you see today you will never see again. The Lord will fight for you; you need only to be still" (Exodus 14:13–14, NIV). In this instance, the Israelites chose to quiet their fear by trusting God, even though the enemy continued to advance. This stillness the Israelites experienced was more of a spiritual reality than a physical one. Similarly, we can be still by bringing our frenetic thoughts and fears to the Lord. Rather than perpetuating hurriedness, we can calm our hurriedness by allowing our hearts and minds to rest in the Lord.

Unlike the Exodus example, stillness can be both a spiritual and physical reality. In fact, spiritual stillness can move us toward physical stillness. When we allow our minds and hearts to be still, we are more able to allow our bodies to be still. But stillness does not only have to be something we aim to do in moments of hurriedness. Stillness can be something we build into our days. It can look like spending a portion of time in the morning to sit quietly with the Lord with no distractions or noise. It can look like taking five minutes before our lunch break is over to pray and take a breath before we resume work again. Or it could look like unplugging all technology and allowing yourself to sit quietly after the day is done. The more we incorporate stillness into our lives, the less we will move hurriedly from one thing to the next. So remember the importance of stillness. Allow yourself the time to stop and be still. You might just find yourself learning to slow down and embracing hush over hurry.

> **WE CAN BE STILL BY BRINGING OUR FRENETIC THOUGHTS AND FEARS TO THE LORD.**

The more we incorporate stillness into our lives, the less we will move hurriedly from one thing to the next.

1. Why is stillness important?

....

....

....

....

....

....

2. What keeps you from being still?

....

....

....

....

....

3. How can you cultivate stillness in your day-to-day life?

....

....

....

....

....

....

The Importance of Prayer

In this booklet, we have discussed the importance of making our relationship with God a priority. You have thought about how you can keep God first in all things, no matter how busy your life becomes. But what does this look like practically? Day 7 of this booklet noted how prayer and Bible study, amid other spiritual disciplines, keep God at the center of our lives and first in our hearts. Today, we will look at the discipline of prayer more deeply and consider how a regular habit of prayer helps us stay rooted amid busyness.

What is prayer? In its basic sense, prayer is communion with God. Prayer is a privilege and a gift because it allows us, as God's children, to talk to our Father anywhere at any time. The incredible blessing of prayer is granted to us through Christ, whose grace and forgiveness unite us with God and give us permanent access to Him. Sometimes when we think of prayer, we think that it involves asking for something from God. And while prayer does involve this, it is not its ultimate purpose. Ultimately, we do not pray to get things from God but to receive more of God. This means that we should view prayer primarily as the means by which we grow in our relationship with God and fellowship with Him.

Unfortunately, busyness can keep us from prayer. When our days are full, we can look down at what we are doing and forget to look up to the God who is over us and with us. We can become so consumed with tasks that we easily forget that we can and should talk to God. When prayer lessens, it becomes more likely for us to try to become self-sufficient. Rather than starting our days with God and depending on Him through prayer as the day continues, we rely on ourselves. We aim to operate in our power and falsely believe that we are capable of running our own lives. But the stress and frustrations we experience from busyness remind us that we need to regularly pray.

First Thessalonians 5:17 tells us to pray constantly, which means to aim to continuously pray to God. Even if something distracts us or takes our concentration for a bit, we are to come back to God and praise Him, talk to Him, or ask Him for help. Regular prayer reminds us of our utter dependence on God. Regular prayer keeps our minds on God and His character, and it encourages us to keep trusting God and looking to Him. This continual communion and fellowship with God eases our racing minds and restless hearts. So, as you aim to be faithful to the Lord with your life and time, remember the importance of prayer. Remember that you are in a relationship with a God who wants to hear from you and speak to you. The more you pray, the more equipped you are to pursue faithfulness to the Lord with diligence and joy.

" ULTIMATELY, WE DO NOT PRAY TO GET THINGS FROM GOD BUT TO RECEIVE MORE OF GOD.

Regular prayer reminds us of our utter dependence on God.

1. *What does your current prayer life look like?*

....

....

....

....

....

2. *How have you seen a lack of prayer impact your life and walk with God negatively?*

....

....

....

....

3. *In what ways can you grow in the discipline of prayer?*

....

....

....

....

....

The Importance of Bible Study

Yesterday, we discussed the importance of prayer, and today, we will discuss the importance of Bible study. Just as a regular rhythm of prayer is essential to our spiritual lives, so is a regular rhythm of Bible study. But, as with prayer, Bible study can be hindered by busyness. As we discussed on day 2, it is possible for us to believe that we do not have enough time for Bible study. We can push it off, thinking that we can do it at a time that is more convenient for us. But if we do not prioritize regular Bible study, our time with God can lessen. And the less time we spend with God in His Word, the more we can believe that we do not need God's Word.

Why, then, do we need God's Word? God gave us Scripture so we could know Him. It is only the Word of God that allows us to know God personally and intimately. As we read and study God's Word, we grow in our knowledge of who God is and what He is about. We grow in our understanding of God's plan of redemption and how Jesus is the fulfillment of this plan. In reading the story of Scripture, we grow more aware of our sin and need for Christ's grace. But the Bible is not just for consumption but application. James 1:22 reminds us that we are to not only be hearers of God's Word but doers. As believers, we are to both listen to and obey Scripture, applying the Bible to our circumstances and obeying what it commands.

Obeying God's Word cultivates faithfulness to the Lord and grows us more into the image of Christ.

Therefore, when we do not read God's Word, our spiritual lives become weak. Just as our bodies need food and water to survive, so do we need God's Word to nourish our souls and help us flourish. One of the reasons we can feel burned out, irritable, and overwhelmed is because we are spiritually running dry. When we feel our attitudes, responses, and emotions growing increasingly negative, we ought to ask ourselves if it is because we have prioritized other things over reading God's Word. If so, realizing our failures in reading God's Word can make us feel ashamed. But God is not angry at us when we fail to spend time with Him in His Word. He does not keep a record of how long we have gone without Bible study. God gives us His grace and welcomes us to come and dwell in His Word. And by His Spirit, He empowers us to prioritize Scripture.

It takes discipline to make Bible study a priority, but this discipline is worthwhile. The more we regularly read God's Word, the more we will grow in our walks with God. The more we will be able to apply truth to our feelings and circumstances. And the more equipped we will be to serve God faithfully. So let us value time in God's Word and feed on it daily.

> " OBEYING GOD'S WORD CULTIVATES
> FAITHFULNESS TO THE LORD
> AND GROWS US MORE INTO
> THE IMAGE OF CHRIST.

God gives us His grace and welcomes us to come and dwell in His Word.

1. *What does your Bible study routine look like?*

....
....
....
....
....
....

2. *What keeps you from regularly reading God's Word?*

....
....
....
....
....
....

3. *How can you discipline yourself to regularly be in God's Word?*

....
....
....
....
....
....

It's Okay to Say "No"

There are moments when saying no is easy. Your dog begs for a bite of chocolate, but you say no because you know chocolate is bad for dogs. Your child asks to eat a cupcake before dinner, but you say no so that they don't spoil their dinner. Declining in these moments feels easy and not guilt-inducing because you know it is for good.

But when it comes to more complicated requests from others, it can feel anything but easy to say no. This difficulty of declining is often rooted in our fear of man. We do not want others to think less of us or accuse us of being rude if we decline an opportunity. We do not want to let others down, so we say yes to avoid hurting our relationships. But saying yes can also be rooted in pride. We might enjoy being the one someone counts on so much that we feel like we always have to agree to requests. When someone brings up an opportunity, we may be quick to say yes so that we can maintain a certain image of selflessness, efficiency, strength, or reliability.

The truth is, saying yes to every request and opportunity only perpetuates busyness. Our schedules can become overfilled, and our relationships can become strained from always agreeing to too many requests and commitments. What are we to do, then, if we struggle to say no? It is helpful to first evaluate the reason we struggle to decline.

Is it out of guilt? Is it out of pride? Whatever our struggle may be, we can bring it to the Lord. We can confess the ways in which we feel shame for declining opportunities or desiring to always say yes out of pride. When we confess these feelings and tendencies to the Lord, we are able to fight against them with God's help. Through the help of the Spirit, we are able to turn away from pride and remove the fear of man.

But even after examining our hearts and confessing to the Lord, we will find ourselves back in a position where we must make a decision to decline or not. For example, perhaps someone from work reaches out with an extra request that we are not sure we can handle. What are we to do? When it comes to making these decisions, it is helpful to ask ourselves, *Is this necessary? Is this something that I can do that will not take away from my other responsibilities and priorities?* Instead of immediately responding, take a moment to consider these questions. Go to God in prayer and ask Him to give you wisdom. Ask the Holy Spirit to grant you discernment. Then respond with what you think is the wisest decision. Remember, you were not made to do it all; therefore, it is okay to say no. Even if you experience guilt for declining, bring your guilt to the Lord and rest in His grace. In fact, the more we rest in God's grace, the more we are able to say no with confidence instead of guilt.

> " YOU WERE NOT MADE TO DO IT ALL;
> THEREFORE, IT IS OKAY TO SAY NO.

The more we rest in God's grace, the more we are able to say no with confidence instead of guilt.

1. *In what ways do you struggle to say no? What is at the root of this struggle?*

....

....

....

....

....

....

2. *Why is it okay to say no?*

....

....

....

....

....

3. *How can you practically discipline yourself to say no when you know it is wise to do so?*

....

....

....

....

....

....

It's Okay to Slow Down

Busyness can be so common in our culture that it almost seems normal. In fact, busyness can often be glorified, depending on where we live. Many cultures praise the person who is busy but put down the person who is not. Sometimes, people who have less on their plate or take more time to rest can be deemed "lazy." Because of this, it is possible for us to feel a level of shame for desiring to slow down. We might even keep ourselves from slowing down and resting because we know we will feel guilty if we do. Regardless of what our culture says and believes, it is not wrong to slow down — it is wise.

Imagine a person going on a journey. He is walking to a different city, and his journey will take him about two days. What would happen if he tried to make this journey without stopping? His body would soon give out. Eventually, he would not be able to go on any further because he did not rest. However, his journey would have been much different if he had allowed himself to rest along the way. Resting would have allowed his body to refuel, and he would have been able to return to his walk strengthened. Similarly, we keep ourselves from being more productive and effective when we do not stop to rest. We may believe that remaining busy keeps us at our best, but in reality, remaining busy keeps us from being our best.

Just like a man taking his time on a journey or like a runner who paces herself so she can keep going, so do we need to pace ourselves by allowing ourselves to slow down. Slowing down gives us the energy we need to pour into our roles and relationships. Slowing down allows us greater motivation and focus in our work. Slowing down enables us to take care of ourselves. Slowing down is for our good. We must not allow what our culture says or makes us feel to keep us from decreasing our pace. Our productivity in the long haul will benefit from intentionally taking our time rather than trying to do it all. Our overall energy and motivation will remain strong and steady instead of worn down and weak.

As the tale of *The Tortoise and the Hare* teaches us, "slow and steady wins the race." It might not feel that way at the moment, but it is true. So when life feels too hectic, remember that it is okay to slow down. When you feel overwhelmed and frazzled, remember that it is okay to breathe and take things one step at a time. If you find yourself struggling to slow down, come to the Lord in prayer and ask for His help. Ask Him to help you not ignore His voice that beckons you to rest. Ask Him to remind you of what is true when you feel ashamed of slowing down. With God's help, your perspective will shift from more and more to little by little.

" WHEN LIFE FEELS TOO HECTIC, REMEMBER THAT IT IS OKAY TO SLOW DOWN.

With God's help, your perspective will shift from more and more to little by little.

1. *What would your life be like if you slowed down more?*

....

....

....

....

....

2. *What are some barriers to slowing down that you experience?*

....

....

....

....

....

3. *What are some practical steps you can take to slow down in your life?*

....

....

....

....

....

It's Okay to Ask for Help

Often, we view those who are independent and self-reliant as strong, whereas we think that those who need and ask for help are weak. Because of this, we can try to be as self-sufficient as possible. We convince ourselves that we must do everything on our own. But when we try to be self-sufficient, we forget that God created us to rely on Him and others. There may be some things we can do in our own strength, but there comes a point when we all need help. Reaching this point is not shameful—it is normal. However, just as we can experience guilt for wanting to slow down, so can we experience guilt for asking for help. We can feel weak and ashamed for needing assistance. But no one person can do everything on their own. The limits we possess as humans mean that we need help, both from God and one another.

Exodus 18 demonstrates how we need the help of others. In this chapter, Moses receives a visit from his father-in-law, Jethro. Jethro watches Moses spend all day giving guidance to the Israelites, and he becomes concerned. When Jethro questions Moses, Moses tells Jethro that it is his responsibility to settle disputes for the people of Israel. Jethro is honest with Moses and tells Moses that he will not only wear himself out but also the people if he continues this way. He advises Moses to be the main advisor and leader for the Israelites but to appoint godly and trustworthy men who can handle minor cases for the Israelites. Jethro wisely recognized that Moses was trying to do too much on his own. In order to take care of himself and the people, Moses needed help. Delegating tasks to a group of men allowed Moses to focus on his role without burning out.

In the same way, we need to reach out to others when we have too much on our plates. When we realize we have hit our limit or cannot do something that is asked of us, it is okay to go to others for help. This might look like asking a co-worker to handle a work task so that you can take a break. It could look like asking your parents to watch your child so that you can clean your home. Or it might look like calling up a friend and requesting their assistance on a project or task so that it is done more efficiently. Asking for help requires humility. It requires us to lay down our pride and admit that we cannot do everything ourselves. But when we take that step and ask for help, we will find that it is what we need. We will find that we are less burned out and more freed up to focus on our priorities. God graciously gives us people we can rely on in our times of need. So let us take up that gift with humility and gratitude and reach out to those God has given us for help.

> " WHEN WE TRY TO BE SELF-SUFFICIENT, WE FORGET THAT GOD CREATED US TO RELY ON HIM AND OTHERS.

God graciously gives us people we can rely on in our times of need.

1. *What is an example of when asking for someone's help was exactly what you needed?*

....

....

....

....

....

2. *In what ways do you struggle to ask for help?*

....

....

....

....

....

3. *What do you need to do in order to rely on others more?*

....

....

....

....

....

....

PART FIVE

Wrapping Up

Day 29 Our Time in Light of Eternity

Day 30 Reflection

Our Time in Light of Eternity

Imagine that you are running a race. You have been running for miles and miles, and although you have felt tired at times, you have persevered. With each mile down, the greater your excitement grows to reach the end. But what if you finished the race and there was no prize? In fact, what if you finished at a dead end? All that running and endurance would seem to be for nothing. Thankfully, this is not our reality as followers of Christ. We do not run toward a goal that has no prize. We do not run in a race that finishes at a dead end. Every believer is running a race that finishes in eternity, and the prize is lasting life with Jesus Christ.

All those in Christ are blessed with an inheritance to come. Because of Christ, we have an inheritance that is "imperishable, undefiled, and unfading, kept in heaven for you" (1 Peter 1:4). We all run toward this end as believers in Christ. However, it is possible for us to forget that we are running toward this end. When we allow ourselves to become too busy, we can take our eyes off of eternity and fix them upon temporary matters. We can end up using our time consumed with things that will ultimately fade away when this life is over.

One day, when you finish your race as a believer, will you be able to look back on your life with contentment? Will you be pleased with the ways in which you used your time for the Lord? Or will you regret that you spent your time on what was temporal rather than eternal? Dwelling on these questions does not have to make us afraid, but these questions should spur us on to action. As believers, we are not to live with our eyes cast down on what is temporary but forward to what is eternal. As Hebrews 12:1b–2a encourages us, "let us lay aside every hindrance and the sin that so easily ensnares us. Let us run with endurance the race that lies before us, keeping our eyes on Jesus, the pioneer and perfecter of our faith." When we keep our eyes fixed upon Jesus, we live with eternity in mind. We let go of what is temporary to focus on what is eternal. We become more encouraged to use our time for God's glory and kingdom. And we are kept from allowing busyness to distract us from our future inheritance.

Our goal as believers is to cross the finish line and hear the words, "Well done, good and faithful servant" (Matthew 25:23). These words will not be the result of endless hustle, worldly gain, or completed to-do lists. They will be the result of a life lived faithfully for the glory of God. So each day, fix your gaze toward the future, and live in light of eternity. Allow what is to come to impact the here and now. And run with grateful endurance.

" WHEN WE KEEP OUR EYES FIXED UPON JESUS, WE LIVE WITH ETERNITY IN MIND.

Each day,
fix your gaze
toward the
future, and
live in light
of eternity.

1. *How does busyness take your gaze away from eternity?*

....

....

....

....

....

....

2. *How does living with eternity in mind affect the ways in which you use your time?*

....

....

....

....

3. *How can you practically live with eternity in mind?*

....

....

....

....

....

Reflection

Congratulations! You have made it to the end of this challenge! You have spent thirty days intentionally evaluating your time and seeking to put an end to perpetual busyness. You have considered your priorities and the truth you need to remember as you aim to live faithfully for the Lord. Through it all, God has been with you. He has been the One strengthening, encouraging, and disciplining you. He deserves all the glory! Now that you have reached the end, take the time to reflect on all that you have learned throughout this challenge. Afterward, say a prayer, thanking God for all that He has done for you through this challenge.

1. *What did this challenge open your eyes to the most?*

   ....

   ....

   ....

   ....

   ....

   ....

2. *Have you seen yourself grow through this challenge?*

   ....

   ....

   ....

....

....

....

3. *In what ways did you grow in your walk with God through this booklet?*

....

....

....

....

....

....

4. *How do you use your time differently now than you did before starting this booklet?*

....

....

....

....

....

5. *What was difficult about this challenge? How did God help you through these difficulties?*

....

....

....

....

....

....

6. *How are you going to live differently in light of this booklet?*

....

....

....

....

....

....

7. *What are some habits you need to keep working on to keep from being too busy?*

....

....

....

....

....

....

8. *What truths do you want to focus on the most as you strive to live faithfully for the Lord?*

....

....

....

....

....

....

9. *How can you continue to lean on the Lord as you
    pursue faithfulness to Him?*

....

....

....

....

....

....

10. *How do you want to live your life in light of eternity?*

....

....

....

....

....

....

*Through it all,
God has been
with you. He has
been the One
strengthening,
encouraging, and
disciplining you.*

BIBLIOGRAPHY

Part One

SWNS. "Why the majority of Americans don't have time to take care of themselves." *New York Post*. October 23, 2019. https://nypost.com/2019/10/23/why-the-majority-of-americans-dont-have-time-to-take-care-of-themselves/.

Part Two

Liu, Grace. "What does the Bible say about the self-care movement?" The Ethics & Religious Liberty Commission of the Southern Baptist Convention. July 5, 2019. https://erlc.com/resource-library/articles/what-does-the-bible-say-about-the-self-care-movement/.

Mills, Andy. "10 Key Points About Work in the Bible Every Christian Should Know." Theology of Work. Accessed July 2, 2022. https://www.theologyofwork.org/resources/what-does-the-bible-say-about-work.

Wedgeworth, Steven. "How Does God Define Family?" Desiring God. July 9, 2021. https://www.desiringgod.org/articles/how-does-god-define-family.

Part Three

Hailey, Logan. "How to Set Boundaries: 5 Ways to Draw the Line Politely." Science of People. Accessed August 10, 2022. https://www.scienceofpeople.com/how-to-set-boundaries/.

Part Four

DeYoung, Kevin. *Crazy Busy: A (Mercifully) Short Book About a (Really) Big Problem*. Wheaton, IL: Crossway, 2013.

*Thank you for studying
God's Word with us!*